OFFICIALLY
WITHDRAWN

Super Simple Things to Do with
Plants

Fun and Easy Science for Kids

Kelly Doudna

Consulting Editor, Diane Craig, M.A./Reading Specialist

A Division of ABDO

ABDO
Publishing Company

To Adult Helpers

Learning about science is fun and simple to do. There are just a few things to remember to keep kids safe. Some activities in this book recommend adult supervision. Some use sharp objects. Be sure to review the activities before starting, and be ready to assist your budding scientist when necessary.

Key Symbols

In this book you will see some symbols. Here is what they mean.

 Adult Help. Get help! You will need help from an adult.

 Sharp Object. Be careful! You will be working with a sharp object.

visit us at www.abdopublishing.com

Published by ABDO Publishing Company, a division of ABDO, P.O. Box 398166, Minneapolis, Minnesota 55439. Copyright © 2011 by Abdo Consulting Group, Inc. International copyrights reserved in all countries. No part of this book may be reproduced in any form without written permission from the publisher. Super SandCastle™ is a trademark and logo of ABDO Publishing Company.

Printed in the United States of America, North Mankato, Minnesota
102010
012011

 PRINTED ON RECYCLED PAPER

Editor: Liz Salzmann
Content Developer: Nancy Tuminelly
Cover and Interior Design and Production: Oona Gaarder-Juntti, Mighty Media, Inc.
Photo Credits: Kelly Doudna, Shutterstock
The following manufacturers/names appearing in this book are trademarks: Arm & Hammer®, McCormick®, Pyrex®

Library of Congress Cataloging-in-Publication Data
Doudna, Kelly, 1963-
   Super simple things to do with plants : fun and easy science for kids / Kelly Doudna.
      p. cm. -- (Super simple science)
   ISBN 978-1-61714-674-9
 1. Plants--Experiments--Juvenile literature. 2. Botany--Experiments--Juvenile literature. 3. Science--Experiments--Juvenile literature. I. Title.
   QK49.D637 2011
   580.78--dc22
                                    2010020860

Super SandCastle™ books are created by a team of professional educators, reading specialists, and content developers around five essential components—phonemic awareness, phonics, vocabulary, text comprehension, and fluency—to assist young readers as they develop reading skills and strategies and increase their general knowledge. All books are written, reviewed, and leveled for guided reading, early reading intervention, and Accelerated Reader® programs for use in shared, guided, and independent reading and writing activities to support a balanced approach to literacy instruction.

Contents

Super Simple Science

Want to be a scientist? You can do it. It's super simple! Science is in things all around your house. Science is in a balloon and in an apple. Science is in seeds and in soil. Science is even in water and in baking soda. Science is everywhere. Try the **activities** in this book. You will find science right at home!

Plants

Learning about science using plants is super simple! Science takes over when you plant a seed. Science happens as roots and leaves grow. Science even happens when you put cut flowers in a vase. In this book, you will see how plants can help you learn about science.

4

Work Like a Scientist

Scientists have a special way of working. It is a series of steps called the Scientific Method. Follow the steps to work like a scientist.

1. Look at something. Watch it. What do you see? What does it do?

2. Think of a question about the thing you are watching. What is it like? Why is it like that? How did it get that way?

3. Try to answer your question.

4. Do a test to find out if you are right. Write down what happened.

5. Think about it. Were you right? Why or why not?

Keep Track

Want to be just like a scientist? Scientists keep notes about everything they do. So, get a notebook. When you do an experiment, write down what happens in each step. It's super simple!

Materials

green bean seeds

knife

small jars

houseplant with runners

clear plastic cups

seeds

potting soil

measuring cup

salt

garlic cloves

baking soda

food coloring

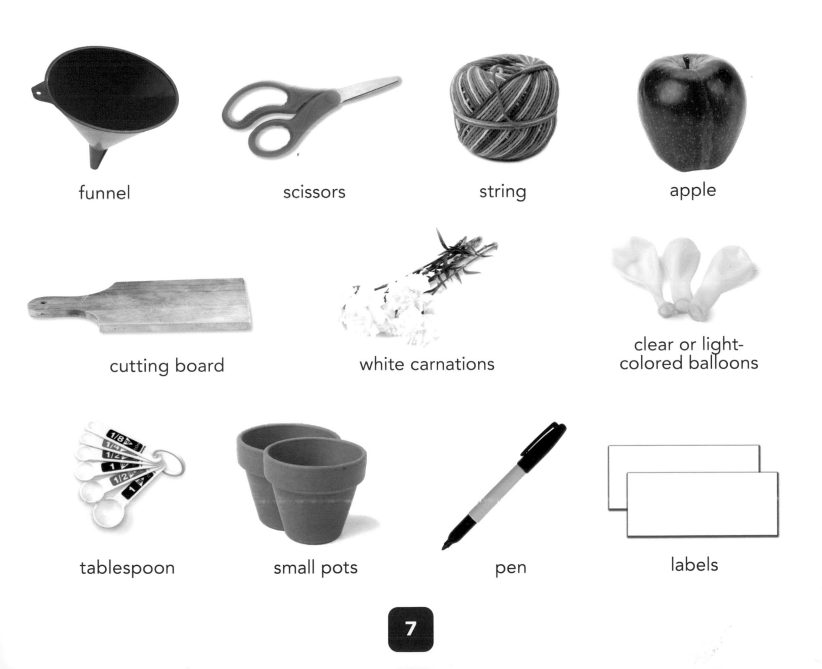

funnel

scissors

string

apple

cutting board

white carnations

clear or light-colored balloons

tablespoon

small pots

pen

labels

Bean There, Done That!

Can you make a bean sprout?

What You'll Need
- clear plastic cup
- potting soil
- 3 green bean seeds
- water

Sprouts grow up.

Sprouts and roots grow out of the seed.

Roots grow down.

1 Fill the cup with potting soil. Use your finger to poke three holes in the soil. The holes should be about 2 inches (5 cm) deep. Make them along the sides of the cup. That way you can see your seeds **sprout**!

2 Drop one seed into each hole. Fill in the holes.

 3 Water the seeds. Put the cup in a warm spot with a lot of light.

4 Water the seeds again when the soil is dry. Look at them every day. What do you see? How do the seeds change?

What's Going On?

Planting a seed is one way to start a new plant. The seed sends roots down into the soil. A sprout grows up toward the light.

New Plant in Town!

Do you always need a seed to grow a new plant?

The plantlet grows roots when left in water.

Before

After

1. Fill the jar about halfway with water.

2. The small plants at the end of the runners on the spider plant are called plantlets. Cut off one plantlet.

3. Put the bottom of the plantlet in the water.

4. Put the jar on a windowsill. Wait two or three weeks. Look at it every day. Make sure the bottom of the plantlet stays underwater. What happens?

5. Plant your plantlet in potting soil. Water it. Now you have a new plant!

What's Going On?

Many kinds houseplants send out runners with plantlets on the ends. When you put a plantlet in water, roots grow from the bottom. Then you can plant it in a pot of dirt. It will keep growing. You don't even need a seed!

11

Get to the Point

Does it matter which
way the point points?

The shoot still
grows up.

Roots still
grow down.

Point Up

Point Down

1 Fill each cup with soil. Poke a hole in the dirt of each cup. Make them along the sides of the cups.

2 Put a **garlic** clove in each hole. In one cup, the clove's point should point up. In the other cup, it should point down.

3 Label the cups POINT UP and POINT DOWN. Cover the cloves with soil.

4 Water both cups. Put them in a bright place. Water the cloves again when the soil is dry.

5 What happens? Does the **sprout** appear at the same time in both cups?

What's Going On?

A garlic clove is a kind of seed called a bulb. A new plant starts from a bulb. The bulb sends a sprout from the pointed end up toward the light. Roots grow down into the soil from the flat end. When the pointed end is down, a sprout still grows up from it. But it takes longer to come out of the dirt.

13

Seed What Happens

How important are light and water to a plant?

The watered seeds sprout.

The dry seeds do nothing.

14

1. Fill each pot with soil.

2. Poke a hole in the soil in each pot.

3. Drop a few seeds in each hole. Cover the seeds with soil.

4. Water one of the pots. Do not water the other pot. Put both pots in a bright place.

5. Check the pots every day. If the soil in the pot that you watered feels dry, add a little water. Do not water the other pot.

6. What happens? Do the seeds in both pots grow?

What's Going On?

Plants and seeds need light and water to grow. The seeds that you watered **sprouted** after a few days. The seeds in the other pot did not.

Balloon Botany

Are balloons good for more than birthday parties?

What You'll Need
- clear or light-colored balloon
- funnel
- measuring cup
- potting soil
- tablespoon
- water
- seeds
- string

The ballon holds in water.

The seeds grow.

1. Blow up the balloon and then let the air out. Do this a few times to **stretch** the balloon.

2. Using the funnel, put ½ cup (118 ml) of soil into the balloon. Pour 4 tablespoons (59 ml) of water into the balloon.

3. Drop a few seeds into the balloon.

4. Blow up the balloon. Tie it closed.

5. Tap the side of the balloon a few times. The soil, water, and seeds should fall to the bottom.

6. Hang the balloon in front of a window. What happens?

What's Going On?

The balloon acts like a greenhouse. It is tied closed so no air can get in. That keeps the water from drying up. It keeps itself watered. The seeds **sprout** just like they would in a pot.

Shrink and Shrivel

How much water is in a plant?

What You'll Need
- apple
- knife
- cutting board
- measuring cup
- baking soda
- salt
- 2 plastic cups

The air draws a lot of water out of the apple.

The salt mixture draws even more water out. This piece is smaller.

Both pieces shrink and shrivel.

18

1 Have your adult helper cut the apple into four pieces. Put one piece into each of the cups. Eat the other two pieces for a healthy snack.

2 Mix together ²/₃ cup (158 ml) salt and ¹/₃ cup (79 ml) baking soda.

3 Pour the salt **mixture** into one of the cups. Make sure the apple is **completely** covered. Leave the other apple piece by itself in the other cup.

4 Let the two cups sit in a dark place for one week. Then take the apple piece out of the salt mixture. Brush it off, but don't rinse it in water. Compare it with the plain apple piece. How do the two pieces look?

What's Going On?

Plants contain a lot of water. The air dries some of the water out of the first apple piece. That causes it to shrivel. The salt mixture pulls even more water out of the other apple piece. That piece becomes smaller than the piece that dried in the air. The water from the apple piece makes the salt mixture stick together.

Carnation Caper

Can you change the color of a flower?

The carnations "drink" the colored water.
They turn the same color as the water.

What You'll Need
- 8 small jars or glasses
- water
- 4 different colors of food coloring
- knife
- cutting board
- 6 white carnations

20

Part 1

1 Fill four jars about half full with water.

2 Add 25 drops of food coloring to each jar. Use a different color in each one.

3 Have your adult helper cut the stems of four flowers. Make the stems about twice as tall as the jars.

4 Put one flower into each jar. Each carnation will drink one color of water. What do you think will happen?

Part 2

 1 Do steps 1 and 2 from Part 1 using the other four jars.

2 Have an adult cut the stems of the last two carnations lengthwise. The cuts should be a little longer than the jars are tall.

3 Place two jars of water next to each other. Put one half of a flower stem in each jar.

4 Do the same for the second carnation and the other two jars.

5 Each of these carnations will drink two colors of water. What do you think will happen this time?

22

Part 3

1 Check all the carnations every few hours. What is happening? How do the carnations that drink one color of water look? How do the carnations that drink two colors of water look? Is there a difference? Do the flowers drink the different colors at the same speed?

What's Going On?

A plant draws water up its stem. It's like what happens when you drink through a straw. The carnation sucks the colored water all the way up to the top. It changes the color of the flower.

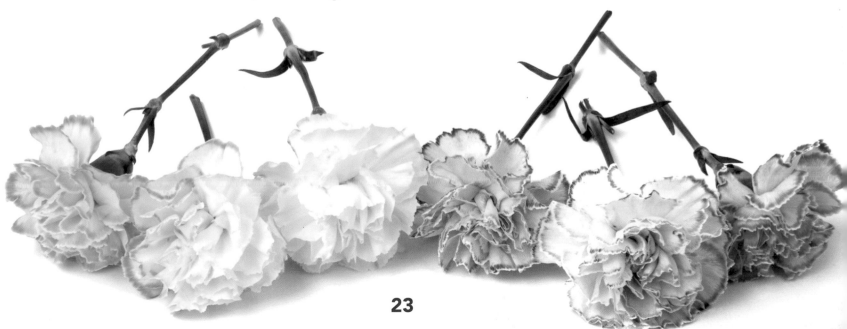

Conclusion

Congratulations! You found out that science can be super simple! And, you did it by growing plants. Keep your thinking cap on. How else can you experiment using plants?

Glossary

activity – something you do for fun or to learn about something.

completely – entirely or in every way.

congratulations – something you say to someone who has done well or accomplished something.

garlic – a plant that grows from a bulb which has a strong smell and taste and is used in cooking.

mixture – a combination of two or more different things.

sprout – 1. to begin to grow. 2. a new plant growing from a seed.

stretch – to get bigger or longer.